SUPER SHEROES OF HISTORY

Indigenous Peoples

Women Who Made a Difference

KATRINA M. PHILLIPS

Children's Press®
An imprint of Scholastic Inc.

Thank you to Brittany Schulman for her insights into Indigenous Peoples' history and culture.

Library of Congress Cataloging-in-Publication Data Available

ISBN 978-1-338-84073-5 (library binding) | ISBN 978-1-338-84074-2 (paperback)

10 9 8 7 6 5 4 3 2 1   23 24 25 26 27

Printed in China   62
First edition, 2023

Series produced for Scholastic by Parcel Yard Press

Contents

Who Are the Super SHEroes of History?

Throughout history, women have ruled countries, led soldiers into battle, changed laws, come up with new ways of thinking, and worked to improve life for everyone. Women's actions and ideas have changed the course of history for whole societies, whole countries, and even the whole world. Women have made a difference. Often, however, their achievements have gone unrecognized.

This book celebrates the life and accomplishments of twelve of these women, twelve Super SHEroes of History! They all belonged to the Indigenous Peoples of North America, and worked to improve the lives of their communities.

Indigenous Peoples are the distinct societies that inhabited a place when outsiders of different cultures or ethnic origins arrived.

SUPER SHEroes
OF HISTORY

Pocahontas

Lozen

Winona LaDuke

Deb Haaland

The Super SHEroes in this book resisted foreign influence, preserved Indigenous traditions, or went into US politics. Some of them were born to leadership, while others gained their reputation through courage or intelligence. Most of them had to overcome many obstacles in order to make their names, but they were still able to achieve things that made a difference to their communities and the times in which they lived.

This book brings the stories of these Super SHEroes to you! And while you read them, remember:

Your story can make a difference, too. You can become a Super SHEro of History!

Pocahontas

Pocahontas's tribe had been living in North America for many centuries when the English **colonists** arrived. Thanks to her role representing her tribe, Pocahontas is the most famous Indigenous woman of early America.

SUPER SHEROES OF HISTORY

Pocahontas was born in the coastal area of what is today the state of Virginia. She was born with the name Matoaka, which means "flower between two streams." Her tribe was one of an **alliance** of tribes known as the Powhatan.

Virginia, shown in this early English map, was home to many groups of Indigenous Peoples.

datafile

Born: c. 1596

Died: 1617

Place of birth: Werowocmoco, now Virginia

Role: Go-between

Super SHEro for: Being an ambassador for her people

The Powhatan lived in villages protected by wooden fences.

This statue of Pocahontas marks her grave in Gravesend, England.

The leader of this alliance was called Wahunsenaca. He was Matoaka's father, so she was an important person in the community.

Little is known about her early life. Her mother may have died in childbirth, so she was probably raised by other women in her family and community. Her mother's name was Pocahontas. Matoaka's father was really sad when his wife passed away, and her daughter reminded him of his lost wife. He started calling his daughter Pocahontas.

In 1607, three ships carrying 104 Englishmen and boys landed on the shores of Virginia. Led by John Smith, they started a **settlement** that they named Jamestown. It was the first permanent English settlement in North America.

The Indigenous Peoples and the colonists did not always get along. Sometimes they traded with each other. But the settlers demanded more and more food and supplies from the Indigenous Peoples. They wanted more land for the settlers that kept coming to Jamestown.

↑ John Smith played a key role in the early history of Jamestown.

Eventually they built an alliance against the Spanish, who had also arrived in the region. Wahunsenaca grew to like John Smith. But the good relations did not last long. These conflicts later turned to war. The First Anglo-Powhatan War began in 1609.

When Matoaka was around fourteen years old, she chose the name Pocahontas in a ceremony and married Kocoum, a young **warrior** from her tribe.

The couple lived in their village until Pocahontas was kidnapped aboard an English ship. She wanted to return to her family. But she was not allowed to leave. She would not see her family for a very long time.

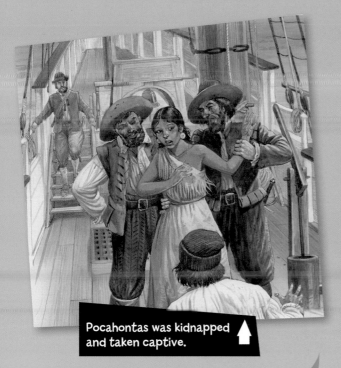

Pocahontas was kidnapped and taken captive.

Did You Know?

There are several versions of Pocahontas's story. This one, based on Pocahontas's tribe's oral history, might be different than the ones you may have heard, read, or watched in a movie. Historical accounts can vary a lot depending on whose point of view they are told from.

When Pocahontas was baptized, she took the name Rebecca.

After a few months with the colonists, Pocahontas was converted to **Christianity**. She also met John Rolfe, an English settler who had brought tobacco seeds to Jamestown. Pocahontas and Rolfe got married. Pocahontas's father could not attend the wedding for fear of being harmed. But he sent a pearl necklace as a wedding gift. Pocahontas later gave birth to a son they named Thomas.

In 1616, Pocahontas, Rolfe, Thomas, and several of her people sailed to England. The English settlers wanted Pocahontas to be seen in England as a symbol of the friendship between the settlers and the Indigenous Peoples. This made her really uncomfortable. Instead, she expressed her unhappiness with the way the colonists treated her people in America.

Pocahontas wanted to return home. In 1617, as she and Rolfe got ready to sail back to America, Pocahontas fell sick and died. Her sister thought she might have been poisoned.

Despite her short life, Pocahontas played a key role in relations between the settlers and the Indigenous Peoples in America.

Pocahontas's son, Thomas, was left in England after his mother died. As an adult, he returned to his tribe and had many children.

What Would You Do?

Pocahontas is said to have been really sad while she was in captivity

How would you feel if somebody did not allow you to see your loved ones?

Life in the Times of Pocahontas
VIRGINIA: 1600s

Pocahontas lived through a time of great change for the Powhatan people.

The Powhatan lived in villages in what is now Virginia. Their homes were constructed by covering a framework of bent **saplings** with woven mats or bark. They grew corn, which they ground up to make flour.

The settlement at Jamestown was protected by a wooden wall.

Powhatan homes were called yehakins.

The men fished in the rivers and hunted in the forests. The women collected nuts, seeds, and berries. The Powhatan were one of many Indigenous Peoples in this region.

The settlers learned from the Powhatan what crops to grow for food.

Later, the English started to take control of Powhatan land to grow tobacco. They wanted to grow their **colony** even more. They burned Powhatan crops and villages, while the Powhatan fought disease brought by settlers and to retain control of their territory. The Powhatan eventually made peace with the English.

The English at Jamestown relied on the Powhatan for food. However, relations between the two sides were often violent. Three wars broke out between the new settlers and the Powhatan between 1609 and 1646. Pocahontas's marriage to John Rolfe helped end the first war in 1614.

After Wahunsenaca died in 1618, Pocahontas's uncle Opechancanough became leader.

Lozen

Lozen was a Chiricahua Apache warrior and **prophet** who fought against US and Mexican forces to defend her people's way of life.

Lozen lived on the San Carlos Reservation in the southwestern United States and northern Mexico. As a young girl, she preferred hunting and horse riding to the traditional work of Apache women, such as weaving or farming.

The San Carlos Reservation was not suited to growing crops for food.

datafile

Born: c. 1840

Died: 1889

Place of birth: Near Ojo Caliente, New Mexico

Role: Warrior and negotiator

Super SHEro for: Fighting for her people's survival

The Apache lived in small homes called wikiups.

Lozen's brother, Victorio, was a great Chiricahua chief and warrior. Lozen decided not to get married. Instead, she would become a warrior like her brother.

Lozen had many skills. She knew how to deliver babies and how to heal people when they were sick or wounded.

A painting on a buffalo skin shows Apaches performing a ritual dance.

15

The San Carlos Reservation was on poor land, and the Apaches struggled to survive. Many wanted to stay on their homelands, where the Apaches had lived before they were forced onto the reservation. In 1877, Victorio led some warriors off the reservation and began to raid settlements in New Mexico. Lozen rode with the warriors.

Lozen became known as a prophet who could communicate with the spirits. US and Mexican soldiers were searching for the Apaches. Apache stories say that if enemy soldiers were nearby, Lozen's palms turned purple as a sign.

This picture shows Lozen's brother, Victorio, who called his sister "a shield to her people."

Lozen risked her life to lead women and children across the Rio Grande.

Apache women were responsible for tasks such as cooking.

When enemies were close, Lozen often led the women and children in Victorio's band to safety. She once guided women and children across the Rio Grande when it was flooding. In 1880, she spent three days helping a young woman and her newborn baby reach safety. Lozen used her knife to hunt for food. She could not use her gun in case soldiers heard her.

Did You Know?

Many Indigenous Peoples traditionally divided roles between men and women. Men were often responsible for hunting, for example, while women grew crops and gathered wild plants and berries, although in some tribes they were also healers. People saw both types of work as having equal value. Lozen was a "two spirit," a spiritual person who did not adhere to binary gender roles.

These Apaches were captured after the Battle of Tres Castillos. ⬆

In 1880, Victorio and almost eighty of his men were killed in a battle in the Tres Castillos Mountains. Some Apache warriors believed they would have won if Lozen had been with them. After Victorio's death, Lozen continued to join Apache attacks and raids. She sometimes led warriors into battle.

After a few months, Lozen joined Geronimo and his people. Geronimo was a famous Apache leader and **medicine man** who refused to surrender to the US military. Lozen fought alongside Geronimo until he was forced to give himself up in 1886.

Geronimo was one of the most feared Indigenous warriors among white Americans. ➡

Lozen and another Apache woman, Dahteste, helped **negotiate** Geronimo's surrender. With Geronimo and the other Apache fighters, they became prisoners of war. They were held in army prisons in Florida and then in Alabama. The conditions in the prisons were terrible.

Lozen died of **tuberculosis** in 1889, while she was still a prisoner. She was buried in an unmarked grave. **She had fought to defend her people during some of the last military clashes between Indigenous Peoples and the US Army.**

US soldiers hold peace talks with Geronimo.

What Would You Do?

Lozen spent most of her life fighting on behalf of her people. She persevered even when times were hard and her own life was at risk.

Who would you make a big sacrifice for?

Would it be your family, your friends, or your whole community?

During the second half of the 19th century, the US government forced the Apaches and many other Indigenous Peoples out of their land and into much smaller territories known as reservations. San Carlos, where Lozen lived, was one of them. The Apaches lacked food and supplies, and they struggled to survive in their new homes.

Apaches dig a large drainage ditch.

After being brought to reservations, Indigenous people had to give up their traditional ways of life. They could not hunt or fish, and they had to rely on the government for supplies.

An Apache woman with a basket for carrying supplies

The reservations were often overcrowded. The soil was usually poor, so the land could not support the number of people who were expected to live there.

Before the Apaches, nobody had lived on the land that became the San Carlos Reservation. There was no grass there, and no animals to hunt. Chiricahua leader Juh called San Carlos the worst place in the whole of the Apaches' homelands in the Southwest. Because of these poor living conditions, some people, like Victorio and Lozen, left the reservation to find a better life.

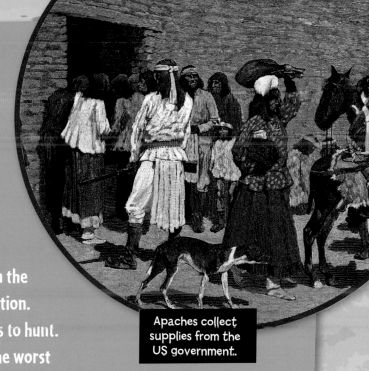

Apaches collect supplies from the US government.

The land on the reservation had few sources of food for the Apaches.

Mary Golda Ross

SUPER
SHEROES
OF HISTORY

Mary Golda Ross was a pioneering Indigenous mathematician and **engineer** who helped the United States fly into space.

Mary was the great-great-granddaughter of John Ross, who had been Principal Chief of the Cherokee Nation. From an early age, she loved learning about math and science. At the time, few girls studied these subjects. Mary was often the only girl in her math classes, and some boys refused to sit next to her.

datafile

Born: August 9, 1908

Died: April 29, 2008

Place of birth: Park Hill, Oklahoma

Role: Mathematician and engineer

Super SHEro for: Being the first female engineer at Lockheed and a key member of the Skunk Works secret project

Mary did not care. She knew she could study what she wanted. The Cherokee had a tradition of giving boys and girls equal education.

At sixteen, Mary started attending a teacher's college, where she majored in math. After she graduated, she taught high school math and science in rural Oklahoma. She worked as a **statistician** for the Bureau of Indian Affairs and as the girls' adviser at the Santa Fe Indian Boarding School in New Mexico.

John Ross led negotiations with the US government to keep the Cherokee in their homelands, but they were forced to move to Oklahoma in the 1830s.

This is the college where Mary studied in Tahlequah, Oklahoma.

Mary was fascinated by what she saw in the night sky. ⬆

Mary wanted to earn a master's degree. She took as many **astronomy** courses as she could and decided she wanted a career linked to space exploration. Her father suggested she move to California to find better opportunities for work.

In the middle of World War II (1939-45), Mary was hired as a mathematician at Lockheed Aircraft Corporation. Mary was part of the team that worked on the P-38 Lightning fighter plane.

A P-38 Lightning fighter plane ⬇

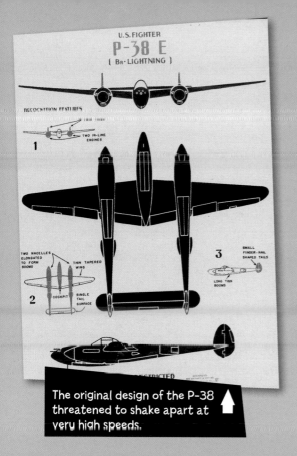

U.S. FIGHTER
P-38 E
(Br·LIGHTNING)

RECOGNITION FEATURES

1 TWO IN-LINE ENGINES

2 TWO NACELLES ELONGATED TO FORM BOOMS
   THIN TAPERED WING
   COCKPIT
   SINGLE TAIL SURFACE

3 SMALL FINGER-NAIL SHAPED TAILS
   LONG THIN BOOMS

The original design of the P-38 threatened to shake apart at very high speeds. ⬆

There was a problem with the plane's original design, and Mary's team had to figure out how the plane could fly safely at high speeds. Mary and the other mathematicians often worked late into the night—and they solved the problem. After the war, Lockheed asked Mary to become one of their engineers. She jumped at the chance and studied to earn the certification she wanted.

Did You Know?

Hundreds of thousands of American women, including Indigenous women, served in World War II. Some served in the military, while others worked in industry to help the war effort. They worked in defense plants, served as radio operators, repaired airplanes, and even helped train antiaircraft artillery gunners.

The United States and the Soviet Union had begun a race to explore space. Lockheed pulled together its forty top engineers for a top-secret project called "Skunk Works." Mary was the only woman on the team aside from the secretary. She was also the only Indigenous person.

As part of this secret project, Mary studied missiles and other defense systems. She helped develop the Agena rocket, which became the basis of the rockets used to explore space. She helped plan future flights to Venus and Mars, and wrote a manual about space flight for astronauts.

◀ The Agena rocket was the forerunner of the rocket that flew humans to the moon in 1969.

Mars ⬆

By the time Mary retired in 1973, she was a senior engineer. She died shortly before her 100th birthday. Much of her work is still **classified**.

Mary has been an inspiration as a pioneering engineer and one of the first Indigenous women to make her name as a scientist.

This painting of Mary is kept in the Smithsonian Museum of the American Indian.

In 2019, Mary was featured on the reverse of a $1 coin.

What Would You Do?

Imagine that you have been given a very important job to do, but there's just one small catch—you can't tell anybody about it.

Could you spend years doing this work while knowing that you might never be recognized for it?

Mary's Cherokee heritage was very important to her. In 2004, when she was ninety-six years old, Mary joined more than 25,000 other Indigenous people in the opening procession of the National Museum of the American Indian in Washington, DC, to celebrate their heritages.

Sequoyah devised a Cherokee alphabet in the 1820s.

The Cherokee believed that boys and girls should have equal access to education. After she retired from Lockheed, Mary spent the next thirty years encouraging young women and young Indigenous people to pursue careers in STEM. She told them that STEM would give them a chance to help their Nation, family, and community—just as it had for her.

The National Museum of the American Indian collects, preserves, and displays the cultures of Indigenous Peoples of the American continent, including the Cherokee Nation. For its opening ceremony, Mary asked her niece to make her a Cherokee dress. It was made of green **calico**, and it was the first traditional dress Mary owned. When she died, Mary left $400,000 to the museum. She believed it was important for the museum to show not only the past of Indigenous Peoples, but also their ongoing story.

The National Museum of the American Indian

Indigenous people in traditional dress parade at the opening of the museum

Deb Haaland

SUPER SHEROES OF HISTORY

Deb Haaland, from the Laguna Pueblo, was one of the first two Indigenous women ever elected to the US Congress.

Both of Deb's parents were in the military. Her father was a Marine and her mother served in the Navy, so the family moved a lot. They later settled in Albuquerque, New Mexico, to be closer to her mother's family. By the time she graduated from high school, Deb had attended thirteen different schools!

The Laguna Pueblo have lived in what is now New Mexico for thousands of years.

datafile

Born: December 2, 1960

Place of birth: Winslow, Arizona

Role: Politician

Super SHEro for: Breaking barriers as an Indigenous politician

Deb earned a law degree in 2006. She ran a small business, and she worked for the San Felipe Pueblo tribal administration. She then started working for the Laguna Pueblo. She became the first woman to run the Laguna Pueblo **gaming** business, which was crucial to their economy. She also helped create environmentally friendly tribal policies.

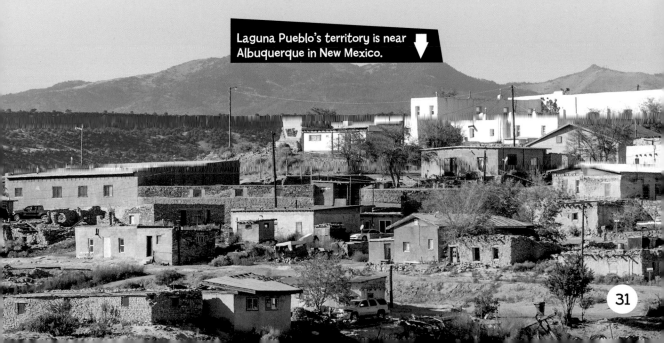

Laguna Pueblo's territory is near Albuquerque in New Mexico.

In 2014, Deb ran as the Democratic candidate for Lieutenant Governor of New Mexico. She didn't win, but she was elected chair of the state Democratic Party. She was the first Indigenous woman to lead a state political party.

In 2018, Deb was elected to the US Congress. She and Sharice Davids, who is Ho-Chunk, were both elected to the House of Representatives. Both women were reelected in 2020.

Deb visits her campaign office during the election in 2018.

Yard signs supporting Deb's election to the House of Representatives

Deb served on a number of important committees during her time in the House of Representatives. She also introduced new laws that centered on Indigenous issues. In 2019, she worked with Senator Elizabeth Warren to put forth a bill to help ensure that the US government keeps the promises it has made to Indigenous Peoples. In 2021, Deb made history again. President Joe Biden appointed her Secretary of the Interior. She became the first Indigenous cabinet secretary in history.

Deb (right) and Sharice Davids, the first two Indigenous women in Congress

Indigenous drummers celebrate the election of Deb and Sharice.

Did You Know?

The Bureau of Indian Affairs was created in 1824, making it one of the oldest parts of the US government. Today it promotes policies and enforces laws to benefit more than 2 million Indigenous people. It also manages millions of acres of land that belong to Indigenous Peoples.

Deb (left) takes the oath of office using a Bible held by her daughter. ⬆

As Secretary of the Interior, Deb became responsible for managing all land and resources owned by the US government. She is in charge of a number of agencies, including the National Park Service and the Bureau of Indian Affairs.

Deb has spent her career helping bring attention to Indigenous issues.

What Would You Do?

Many Indigenous people strive to create change and work to help their communities. They might serve in tribal government positions or work for local or national organizations.

What kinds of problems do you see around you?

What could you do to make a difference?

Although the Secretary of the Interior helps manage tribal land, Indigenous Peoples are able to use their resources in different ways. The Menominee in Wisconsin, for example, have been logging since the nineteenth century. The lumber industry helps support the community. The Menominee focus on sustainable forest management practices.

Other Indigenous Peoples provide for their people through gaming.

Tribes such as the Navajo provide private schools for young people.

The Indian Gaming Regulatory Act, passed in 1988, allows for gambling on reservations. Gambling profits help fund tribal education, health care, and programs to preserve Indigenous languages and cultures.

The Menominee carefully preserve their forests.

Indigenous Peoples
CHEROKEE

Nanyehi

Nanyehi
(1738-1822)

Nanyehi, also known as Nancy Ward, was a Cherokee from what is now Tennessee. Cherokee women played important roles in tribal affairs, like deciding when to go to war. Women such as Nanyehi often fought alongside their husbands and brothers. After her first husband, Kingfisher, was killed in battle in 1755, Nanyehi grabbed his gun and kept fighting. Her bravery earned her the title "Beloved Woman." She was highly respected both by her people and by the white settlers. Nanyehi spent much of her life calling for peace between settlers and Indigenous Peoples.

Queen Lili'uokalani

Lili'uokalani was born Lydia Kamakaeha to one of Hawaii's high-ranking Indigenous families. Her brother was chosen as king in 1874, and Lydia became his heir. She took the royal name Lili'uokalani and toured the world representing Hawaii. She became Hawaii's first queen after the king died in 1891. US influence in Hawaii was growing, and Lili'uokalani led resistance against the illegal **annexation** of the islands by the United States. In 1895, politicians who supported the US annexation put some of the queen's supporters in jail. In order to protect them, she agreed to give up her throne. Annexation followed in 1898. The first and last queen of Hawaii, she is remembered as an inspiring leader of her people. She also wrote a popular song, "Aloha Oe," or "Farewell to Thee," which some see as a sad farewell to Hawaii's independence.

Queen Lili'uokalani
(1038–1917)

Indigenous **Peoples**
NORTHERN PAIUTE

Sarah Winnemucca

Sarah Winnemucca grew up with remarkable language skills that led her to become a spokesperson and **advocate** for her people. She served as an interpreter for the US Army, but she also spoke out about the conditions in which the Paiute were forced to live. She gave lectures across the country to raise awareness about the problems faced by Indigenous Peoples. Published in 1883, *Life Among the Paiutes* was the first **autobiography** written by an Indigenous woman. Sarah continued to advocate for her people until her death. By the time she died, she was one of the most famous Indigenous women of the nineteenth century.

Sarah Winnemucca
(c. 1844–1891)

Indigenous
Peoples
OJIBWE

Maude Kegg

Born near the Mille Lacs Indian Reservation in Minnesota, Maude Kegg started learning beadwork when she was a child. She spent her life working to keep Ojibwe stories, crafts, and language alive. She later earned national recognition for her work, and her **bandolier** bags are displayed in a number of museums, including the Smithsonian, as outstanding examples of traditional beadwork.

Maude Kegg
(1904-1996)

Winona LaDuke

Winona LaDuke is an advocate for Indigenous people and the environment. Throughout their history, Indigenous Peoples have lived in harmony with the natural world. Winona argues that traditional Indigenous ways of using the land and its resources should be the basis of our modern efforts to preserve the environment.

Indigenous
Peoples
OJIBWE

Winona LaDuke
(born 1959)

SUPER SHEROES
OF HISTORY

Indigenous
Peoples
MUSCOGEE

Joy Harjo

Joy Harjo
(born 1951)

In 2019, Joy Harjo, from the Muscogee Nation, was the first Indigenous person to be named US Poet Laureate. She is also only the second Poet Laureate to serve three terms in the position. She published her first book of poetry in 1975, and her Indigenous heritage inspires much of her work. Joy has written books of poetry, memoirs, and children's books. She is also a musician, screenwriter, playwright, and producer. Joy has won many awards for her work, and she performs nationally and internationally.

Indigenous
Peoples
SPOKANE

Charlene Teters

Charlene Teters
(born 1952)

When Spokane artist Charlene Teters took her children to a University of Illinois basketball game, she was horrified that the team had an Indigenous person as a mascot. Teters started going to games with a sign that said "Indians Are Human Beings Not Mascots." The college eventually dropped the mascot. Teters has gone on to lead efforts to get rid of racist sports mascots across the country.

Lori Piestewa

Lori Piestewa's family has a history of military service. A member of the Hopi Tribe, Lori served in Iraq and was the first Indigenous woman to die in combat overseas. Arizona's Piestewa Peak is named in her honor, and she was **posthumously** awarded the Purple Heart, an award for people wounded or killed in military service.

Indigenous
Peoples
HOPI

Lori Piestewa
(1979–2003)

Timeline

Here are some highlights in the lives of Indigenous Super SHEroes.

SUPER SHEroes OF HISTORY

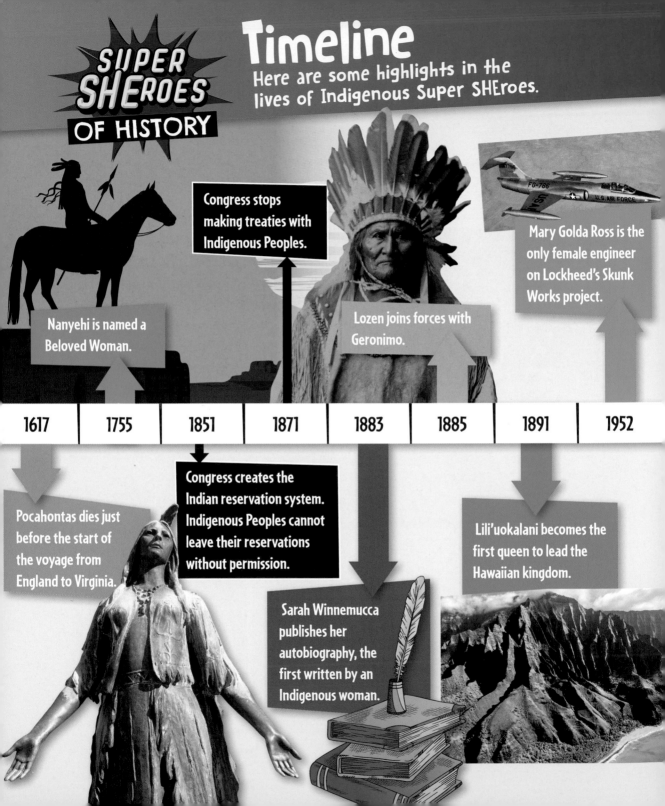

Congress stops making treaties with Indigenous Peoples.

Mary Golda Ross is the only female engineer on Lockheed's Skunk Works project.

Nanyehi is named a Beloved Woman.

Lozen joins forces with Geronimo.

| 1617 | 1755 | 1851 | 1871 | 1883 | 1885 | 1891 | 1952 |

Pocahontas dies just before the start of the voyage from England to Virginia.

Congress creates the Indian reservation system. Indigenous Peoples cannot leave their reservations without permission.

Lili'uokalani becomes the first queen to lead the Hawaiian kingdom.

Sarah Winnemucca publishes her autobiography, the first written by an Indigenous woman.

Charlene Teters begins her campaign against racist Indigenous mascots in sports.

Piestewa Peak is renamed in honor of Lori Piestewa, the first Indigenous woman to die in combat overseas.

Deb Haaland is confirmed as the Secretary of the Interior, making her the first Indigenous Cabinet secretary in US history.

| 1989 | 1991 | 2004 | 2008 | 2019 | 2021 |

Vinona LaDuke begins a project to protect the environment.

The National Museum of the American Indian opens in Washington, DC.

Joy Harjo is the first Indigenous person to be named US Poet Laureate.

Where in the World?

1. Deb Haaland
Washington, DC
As Secretary of the Interior, Deb Haaland oversees the US Department of the Interior, which was created in 1849 and is based in Washington, DC.

2. Joy Harjo
Tulsa, Oklahoma
Born in Tulsa, Oklahoma, Joy Harjo has traveled around the world as a poet and as a musician.

3. Maude Kegg
Mille Lacs Indian Reservation
The Mille Lacs Indian Reservation, where Maude Kegg lived, was created in 1855 as home to the Mille Lacs Band of Ojibwe.

4. Winona LaDuke
White Earth Indian Reservation, Minnesota
Winona LaDuke belongs to the White Earth Indian Reservation in northern Minnesota.

5. Queen Lili'uokalani
Honolulu, Hawaii
'Iolani Palace in Hawaii was the official residence of Lili'uokalani and the monarchs who ruled before her.

6. Lozen
San Carlos Reservation, New Mexico
Led by Lozen's brother, Victorio, some Apaches fled the horrible conditions at the San Carlos Reservation in 1877.

7. Nanyehi

Ball Ground, Georgia

Nanyehi fought alongside her husband, Kingfisher, in the 1755 Battle of Taliwa in Ball Ground, Georgia.

9. Pocahontas

Jamestown, Virginia

After being kidnapped by an English colonist, Pocahontas was held captive in Jamestown.

10. Mary Golda Ross

Burbank, California

Mary was the only female engineer to join the top-secret Lockheed Skunk Works project in Burbank.

11. Charlene Teters

Urbana-Champaign, Illinois

After attending a basketball game at the University of Illinois, Charlene started protesting the school's use of a racist Indigenous mascot.

8. Lori Piestewa

Piestewa Peak, Arizona

Piestewa Peak in Arizona was named in honor of fallen soldier Lori Piestewa in 2008, five years after her death in Iraq.

12. Sarah Winnemucca

Humboldt Lake, Nevada

In 2005, the state of Nevada sent a statue of Sarah, who was born in Humboldt Lake, to the US Capitol.

Glossary

advocate (**ad**-vuh-kit) someone who supports a particular cause

alliance (uh-**lye**-uhns) an agreement to work together to achieve a goal

annexation (a-nek-**say**-shuhn) the act of taking over a country by force

astronomy (uh-**strah**-nuh-mee) a branch of science that studies space and celestial objects

autobiography (aw-toh-bye-**ah**-gruh-fee) a book in which the author tells the story of their own life

bandolier (ban-duh-**leer**) a shoulder bag with a wide strap, often decorated with beadwork

calico (**kal**-i-*koh*) cotton cloth printed with a colorful pattern

Christianity (*kris*-chee-**an**-i-tee) the religion based on the life and teachings of Jesus Christ

classified (**klas**-uh-fide) declared secret by an authority

colonists (**kah**-luh-nists) people who live in a colony or help establish a colony

colony (**kah**-luh-nee) a territory settled by people from another place

engineer (*en*-juh-**neer**) someone who designs and builds machines or structures

gaming (**gay**-ming) casinos, bingo halls, and other gambling operations that operate on tribal lands

medicine man (**med**-i-sin man) someone believed to have magical powers of healing

negotiate (ni-**goh**-shee-*ate*) to bargain to make an agreement

posthumously (**pahs**-chuh-muhs-lee) occurring after death

prophet (**prah**-fit) a person who is thought to speak to the gods and know the future

reservation (*rez*-ur-**vay**-shuhn) land set aside for Indigenous Peoples through treaties or other agreements

ritual (**rich**-oo-uhl) a series of actions always repeated the same way as part of a religious ceremony

saplings (**sap**-lingz) young trees

settlement (**set**-uhl-muhnt) a place where people establish a community

statistician (*sta*-tuh-**sti**-shuhn) someone who studies large quantities of information, such as numbers

tuberculosis (tu-*bur*-kyuh-**loh**-sis) an infectious disease that mainly affects the lungs

warrior (**wor**-ee-ur) a brave and experienced fighter

Index

Further Reading

Smith, John L. *Sarah Winnemucca: A Princess for the People (Fields of Silver and Gold)*. Reno, NV: Keystone Canyon Press, 2020.

Sorell, Traci. *Classified: The Secret Career of Mary Golda Ross, Cherokee Aerospace Engineer*. Minneapolis, MN: Milbrook Press, 2021.

Sullivan, Laura L. *Pocahontas (Inside Guide: Famous Native Americans)*. New York: Cavendish Square Publishing, 2021.

About the Author

Katrina Phillips grew up in northern Wisconsin. She earned her BA and PhD in history, and she's now a writer and history professor. As an Ojibwe woman, she loved writing about these Super SHEroes of history—especially because they all made or are making a difference in their own ways! When she's not writing, researching, or teaching, she and her husband spend most of their free time wrangling their two sons and their dog. She loves chocolate, crocheting, and crossword puzzles.

About the Consultant

Bonnie Morris grew up in California, North Carolina, and Washington, DC. She earned her PhD in women's history and is the author of nineteen books, including *Women's History For Beginners*, *The Feminist Revolution*, and *What's the Score? 25 Years of Teaching Women's Sports History*. She is also a scholarly adviser to the National Women's History Museum and a historical consultant to Disney Animation. In one of her favorite jobs as a professor, she lived on a ship and went around the world (three times!) teaching for Semester at Sea. She has kept a journal since she was twelve and has filled more than 200 notebooks using a fountain pen.